Chefs' Special

Favourite Indian Desserts

Chefs' Special

Favourite Indian Desserts

Compiled by Master Chefs of India

Lustre Press
Roli Books

A Taste of Indian Desserts

Most Indians love sweets, and India has a plethora of sweets of every kind to suit every palate. The art of making delicious sweets and desserts has been the preserve of generations of temple cooks and *halwais* (sweetmakers). And today, as always, giving sweets conveys gratitude, affection and joy.

This book is not just a cookbook, chock-a-block with recipes, but contains carefully selected sweets and desserts that will put the finishing touch to any meal. With more than 60 traditional specialities, this book illustrates the diversity of regional cooking styles. Divided into four sections, the first section covers easy-to-make confections such as coconut *burfee* (fudge), *besan ladoo* (sweet gram flour balls), *sandesh* (creamy cheese fudge), and so forth. *Sandesh* first made its appearance in Calcutta. The ever-popular *sandesh* is made from sweetened *chenna* (soft cottage cheese), rolled into a ball or flattened into a disc (small wooden and stone-carved moulds), and emerges as conch shells or other shapes. Colour and flavour is added according to taste. You will find your favourites in the hot and cold desserts section, which includes a wide array of sumptuous delights, made not only during festivals, but also on holidays. From milk-white *rasgullas* (cottage cheese dumplings) swimming in bowls of syrup to *rajbhogs* (cardamom-stuffed cheese dumplings) and *chenna payas* (cottage cheese dumplings in thickened milk), all the regional delicacies are there, just waiting for you to make them.

Last, but not least, is a section on nutritious, low-calorie desserts which will delight the hearts of all calorie and health-conscious people.

Basic Preparations

Soft cottage cheese (*chenna*): For about 400 gm; boil 2 lt milk in a deep pot and remove from the fire. Add 60 ml vinegar or lemon juice till the milk curdles. Transfer the curdled milk into a muslin cloth to drain out the whey. Use either in crumbled form or else wrap in a muslin cloth and press down with a weight for half an hour or so. This will form into a block, which can then be cut to desired size pieces.

Yoghurt (*dahi*): If you want to set yoghurt at home buy starter from any store or sweet shop.
Heat 1 lt of milk till it is warm to touch. Add 2 tsp of yoghurt to it and stir well. Transfer to a clay pot, cover with a lid and then keep in a warm place to allow it to set. In winter, it usually takes longer to set and also needs to be kept warmer than usual. In the summer months, it sets in a relatively short time.

Wholemilk fudge (*khoya*): Boil 800 ml of full-cream milk in a heavy-bottomed pan. Cook until all the moisture has evaporated and the milk solids are left behind. Stir constantly and scrape from all the sides till a thick paste-like consistency is obtained.

Clarified butter (*ghee*): Melt some unsalted butter in a wok (*kadhai*); cook till it froths. Remove the scum that collects on the top and pour the melted butter in another container. Keep aside to cool. Discard the fat that rises to the top, leaving the clarified butter behind.

Gram flour (*besan*): Usually, gram flour cannot be substituted with any other flour as it has its own distinctive flavour. Many Indian desserts are made of gram flour. Roast the Bengal gram (*chana dal*) in a pan, stirring constantly, so that they do not burn. Remove the pan from the heat and cool. Then blend in a blender, sieve and store in an airtight container.

Coconut (*nariyal*) milk: Grate 1 coconut and add 200 ml of hot water. Blend the mixture for 8-10 minutes. Strain the coconut mixture through a muslin cloth. This is the first extract.

Repeat the same procedure with the remaining coconut and 200 ml of water. Strain again to get the second extract.

Repeat again with 200 ml of water to get the third extract.

Lavang Latika
Bengali clove-flavoured flour crispies

Preparation time: 1 hr.
Cooking time: 1½ hrs.
Serves: 4-6

Ingredients:

Refined flour (*maida*)	1 cup / 200 gm
Saffron (*kesar*), soaked	
in 1 tbsp water	a few strands
Oil	2 tbsp / 30 ml
Water	4 tbsp / 60 ml
For the filling:	
Wholemilk fudge (*khoya*),	
mashed (see p. 6)	¾ cup / 150 gm
Almonds (*badam*), slivered	4 tsp / 20 gm
Pistachios (*pista*), slivered	4 tsp / 20 gm
Clove (*laung*) powder	½ tsp / 3 gm
Sugar, powdered	2 tbsp / 30 gm
For the sugar syrup:	
Sugar	2½ cups / 500 gm
Water	3½ cups / 700 ml
Cloves (*laung*)	12
Oil for frying	

Method:

1. Sieve the flour and make a well in the centre.
2. Add the saffron and oil. Mix well. Add the water and knead to make a hard dough. Cover the dough with a moist cloth and keep aside for 15-20 minutes.
3. For the filling, mix the wholemilk fudge, almonds, pistachios, clove powder and sugar together. Divide the filling into 12 equal portions.
4. For the sugar syrup, boil the water with sugar till the sugar dissolves completely.
5. Divide the dough into 12 equal portions and shape

each portion into balls. Roll out each ball into 6"-diameter pancakes.

6. Place one portion of the filling in the centre of each pancake and brush the edges with water. Fold the pancakes from one side to the centre and press firmly to seal in the filling. Repeat from the other side to give a 2" wide strip.

7. Keeping the folded side out, make a ring with the strip. Brush the edges with water, press them firmly down to the centre to form squares. Seal each square with a clove.

8. Heat the oil in a wok (*kadhai*); shallow fry the squares on a very low heat till crisp and golden brown. Remove with a slotted spoon and drain the excess oil.

9. Submerge these crispies in hot sugar syrup completely, turning gently. If required, soak for 2-3 minutes. Remove and serve.

Sweetener

Add a pinch of soda bicarbonate while making sugar syrup to prevent it from crystallising or forming a crust.

Kesar Sandesh

Saffron-cheese fudge

Preparation time: 20 min.
Cooking time: 2 hrs.
Serves: 2-4

Ingredients:

Saffron (*kesar*)	½ tsp / 3 gm
Full-cream milk	1½ cups / 300 ml
Lemon (*nimbu*) juice	4 tbsp / 60 ml
Sugar, powdered	½ cup / 100 gm

Method:

1. Roast the saffron in a dry pan and pound to a fine powder. Dissolve in 2 tbsp hot milk. Keep aside.
2. Heat the full-cream milk in a pan over a high heat; bring to a frothing boil, stirring continuously. Reduce the heat and add the lemon juice to curdle the milk. If the milk does not curdle, then add 1 more tbsp of lemon juice. Remove from the heat and set aside to cool.
3. Pour the cheese-whey mixture into a moist cheesecloth. Pick up the cheesecloth by its corners, twist it loosely just to seal the cheese inside and rinse under the tap for a few minutes. Hang the cloth for 20-30 minutes to allow the excess water to drain.
4. Remove the cheese on a clean work surface and crumble till it becomes fluffy and even. Blend in the sugar and knead till smooth and grainless.
5. Transfer the cheese-sugar mixture to a heavy-bottomed pan. Cook for 10-15 minutes until the mixture becomes a little thick and glossy.

6. Divide the mixture into two portions. Mix the dissolved saffron into one portion till it turns yellow. Divide the yellow cottage cheese mixture into 2 portions again.

7. Spread three alternate layers of yellow, white and yellow mixture on a buttered tray to form a 2"-thick cake. Keep aside to cool and then cut into 1½"-thick squares. Arrange on a platter and serve.

Nourishing Nutrient
*Keep milk away from sunlight to prevent
any loss in its vitamin B content.*

⁓

Gur Sandesh
Jaggery-cheese fudge

Confectionery

Ingredients:

Soft cottage cheese (*chenna*)	500 gm
Sugar	7½ tbsp / 80 gm
Jaggery (*gur*)	7½ tbsp / 80 gm

Method:

1. Prepare the soft cottage cheese (see p. 6); hang it in a muslin cloth to drain the excess water.
2. Divide the cottage cheese into two portions; mix sugar into one portion and jaggery into the other.
3. Cook both the mixtures separately till they become dry and powdery. Keep aside to cool.
4. Combine both the mixtures, mix well and make small round balls.
5. Put the balls in small fudge moulds and press so that the balls takes the shape of the moulds. Serve cold. Can be kept refrigerated for up to 4 days.

Besan Ladoo
Sweet gram flour balls

Preparation time: 30 min.
Cooking time: 40 min.
Makes: 2 dozen

Ingredients:

Gram flour *(besan)*, sifted	1 cup / 200 gm
Clarified butter	¾ cup / 150 gm
Coconut *(nariyal)*, dried, grated	2 tbsp / 30 gm
Walnuts *(akhrot)*, chopped	2 tbsp / 30 gm
Nutmeg *(jaiphal)*, ground	a pinch
Sugar	½ cup / 100 gm

Method:

1. Melt the clarified butter in a heavy-bottomed pan over a moderate heat. Add the gram flour, coconut and walnuts (keep some aside for garnishing) and nutmeg. Cook for 5 minutes; stirring constantly.
2. Add the sugar and continue to cook for 15 minutes or until the mixture is thick and golden brown.
3. Transfer the mixture to a clean, flat surface. When cool enough, shape into 24 equal-sized balls.
4. Garnish with the remaining coconut and walnuts and serve. (You can store these for 10-15 days.)

Coconut Burfee

Coconut fudge

Preparation time: 10 min.
Cooking time: 10 min.
Serves: 4

Ingredients:

Coconut (*nariyal*) powder	3 cups / 600 gm
Sugar	4 tbsp / 60 gm
Water	1/3 cup / 80 ml
Essence (sweet *ittar*)	1 drop
Saffron (*kesar*)	a few strands
Green cardamom (*choti elaichi*) powder	1 tsp / 5 gm
Pistachios (*pista*) or silver leaf (*varq*) for garnishing	

Method:

1. Heat the sugar and water in a pan. Stir continuously till the sugar is completely dissolved.
2. Bring the sugar syrup to a boil. Add the coconut powder, sweet *ittar*, saffron and green cardamom powder. Mix well.
3. Remove from the heat and spread evenly on a greased baking tray. Cool and cut into 8 pieces.
4. Garnish with pistachios or silver leaf.

Zebre
Nepalese sweetened rice rings

Preparation time: 1 hr.
Cooking time: 20 min.
Serves: 2-4

Ingredients:

Rice	1¼ cups / 250 gm
Cream (*malai*) or butter	1½ tbsp / 20 gm
Milk	½ cup / 100 ml
Jaggery (*gur*), ground	50 gm
Water as required	
Oil or clarified butter for frying	

Method:

1. Clean the rice and soak it in cold water for about an hour.
2. Drain and grind to a coarse paste.
3. Add the cream or butter, milk and molasses and mix thoroughly.
4. Gradually, add water to the rice mixture to get a thin consistency. Put aside for 15-20 minutes.
5. Heat the oil / clarified butter in a flat-bottomed pan. Place a medium-sized steel bowl upside down in the middle of the oil.
6. When the oil is smoking hot, take one ladleful of the batter and pour it slowly all around the bowl to make a ring.

7. Alternatively, you can use a coconut shell with a hole to pour the batter.
8. Cook till the ring becomes brown in colour; then turn and cook the other side too. The oil must be very hot and the ring should be turned quickly and removed from the oil as soon as it is done.
9. Make similar rings and cook till all the batter is used up.
10. Serve hot or cold.

Milk Matters
Add a drop of glycerine to the milk while boiling to prevent it from spilling.

Bambaison

Nepalese cardamom-flavoured milk sweet

Preparation time: 15 min.
Cooking time: 30 min.
Serves: 2-4

Ingredients:

Wholemilk fudge (*khoya*), grated (see p. 6)	1 kg
Clarified butter (*ghee*)	¾ cup / 150 gm
Sugar	1¼ cups / 250 gm
Milk	½ cup / 100 ml
Green cardamom (*choti elaichi*) powder	1 tsp / 5 gm

Method:

1. Heat the clarified butter in a heavy-bottomed pan. Add the wholemilk fudge and cook over a medium flame, stirring continuously till light golden.

2. Add the sugar and milk; continue stirring till the sugar dissolves. Keep cooking over a medium flame till the wholemilk fudge becomes a lumpy mass and leaves the sides of the pan.

3. Remove from the flame and mix in the green cardamom powder. Grease a flat plate with clarified butter and transfer the cooked lump on to it. Spread it out with a greased spatula or the back of a serving spoon. Cut into pieces when still hot. Remove from the plate only when it cools.

Anarasa
Nepalese rice flour delicacy

Preparation time: 5 hrs.
Cooking time: 20 min.
Serves: 2-4

Ingredients:

Rice flour, finely ground	2 cups / 400 gm
Sugar	1 cup / 200 gm
Lemon (*nimbu*) juice	4 tsp / 20 ml
Gingelly seeds (*safed til*)	½ cup / 100 gm
Clarified butter (*ghee*)	1¼ cups / 250 gm

Method:

1. Mix together the rice flour, sugar and lemon juice. Collect in a heap, cover with a deep dish turned upside down. Keep aside for 4-5 hours. Remove the dish and knead the mixture into a dough with a little water.
2. Sprinkle the gingelly seeds on a flat steel plate.
3. Make small lemon-sized balls of the dough and place on the gingelly seeds. With your fingers press the balls to form flat rounds, about 5"-diameter.
4. Heat some clarified butter in a flat pan; fry the rice rounds, with the gingelly seeds on top, till they become light brown. Keep spooning the clarified butter (from the pan itself) over the rounds, but do not turn them over. Remove with a slotted spoon and drain on absorbent kitchen towels.

Badam Halwa
Almond delight

Preparation time: I hr.
Cooking time: 30 min.
Serves: 4-5

Ingredients:

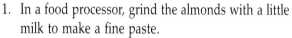

Almonds (*badam*), blanched, chopped	2½ cups / 500 gm
Clarified butter (*ghee*)	1 cup / 200 gm
Milk	1 cup / 200 ml
Sugar	2½ cups / 500 gm
Green cardamom (*choti elaichi*) powder	1 tsp / 5 gm
Saffron (*kesar*)	¼ tsp / 1½ gm
Silver leaf (*varq*), optional	

Method:

1. In a food processor, grind the almonds with a little milk to make a fine paste.
2. Heat the clarified butter in a heavy-bottomed pan. Add the almond paste and cook over a medium heat until light golden.
3. Add the milk and sugar, cook over a medium heat for 10-15 minutes till the moisture evaporates and the mixture becomes thick. Remove from the heat.
4. Add the green cardamom powder and saffron.
5. To serve cold, spread on a greased flat tray, cut into small squares and decorate with silver leaf. To serve hot, ladle individual portions on to dessert plates and decorate with silver leaf.

Gajar Ka Halwa
Shredded carrot pudding

Preparation time: 40 min.
Cooking time: 1 hr.
Serves: 10-12

Ingredients:

Carrots, washed, peeled, shredded	1 kg
Milk	3 cups / 600 ml
Sugar	½ cup / 100 gm
Brown sugar	5½ tbsp / 85 gm
Green cardamom	
(*choti elaichi*) powder	1 tsp / 5 gm
Clarified butter (*ghee*)	5 tbsp / 80 gm
Almonds (*badam*), slivered	2 tbsp / 30 gm
Raisins (*kishmish*)	2½ tbsp / 40 gm
Walnuts (*akhrot*), chopped	2½ tbsp / 40 gm
Cloves (*laung*), ground	¼ tsp / 1½ gm
Nutmeg (*jaiphal*), ground	¼ tsp / 1½ gm
Cinnamon (*dalchini*), ground	¼ tsp / 1½ gm

Method:

1. Mix the carrots and milk in a pan and bring to a boil. Reduce the heat to moderate and cook for 20-25 minutes, stirring continuously, till the mixture is nearly dry.
2. Add both the sugars and half of the green cardamom powder, stirring continuously. Cook for 10-12 minutes. Remove the pan from the heat and keep aside.
3. Heat the clarified butter in another pan over a moderate heat; fry the almonds until golden. Stir in the carrot mixture and the raisins, walnuts and ground spices. Cook till the mixture begins to separate from the sides.
4. Serve hot, garnished with remaining cardamom.

Moong Dal Halwa
Fried green gram pudding

Preparation time: 40 min.
Cooking time: 20 min.
Serves: 4

Ingredients:

Split green gram (*moong dal*), washed,
   soaked for 30 minutes   ½ cup / 100 gm
Clarified butter (*ghee*)   2 tbsp / 30 gm
Sugar   4 tbsp / 60 gm
Water   ½ cup / 100 ml
Green cardamoms (*choti elaichi*)   2
Cashew nuts (*kaju*), broken   2 tsp / 10 gm
Wholemilk fudge (*khoya*),
   grated (see p. 6)   ¼ cup / 5 0 gm
Pistachios (*pista*), chopped   10

Method:

1. Drain the split green gram and grind into a rough paste.
2. Heat the clarified butter in a wok (*kadhai*) and fry the green gram paste till light golden in colour.
3. Boil the sugar and water in another pan. Stir continuously till the sugar dissolves completely. Boil rapidly for 5 minutes. Add to the fried paste.
4. Cook, stirring vigorously, till the mixture becomes thick. Add the green cardamom powder.
5. Garnish with cashew nuts, wholemilk fudge and pistachios. Serve hot.

Suji Ka Halwa
Semolina pudding

Preparation time: 15 min.
Cooking time: 30 min.
Serves: 2-4

Ingredients:

Semolina (*suji*)	1 cup / 200 gm
Clarified butter (*ghee*)	¾ cup / 150 gm
Sugar	1 cup / 200 gm
Milk	4 cups / 800 ml
Green cardamoms (*choti elaichi*)	1 tsp / 5 gm
Almonds (*badam*)	¼ cup / 50 gm
Saffron (*kesar*)	a pinch

Method:

1. Heat the clarified butter in a wok (*kadhai*); add the semolina and fry on a low heat till the colour changes to light brown.
2. Add the sugar, milk, green cardamoms, almonds, raisins and saffron. Cook till the mixture becomes thick and the clarified butter shows on the surface.
3. Serve hot.

Anti-drive
*To keep ants away from sugar,
put some cloves in the sugar container.*

Mithe Pille Chawal

Sweetened yellow rice

Preparation time: 15 min.
Cooking time: 20 min.
Serves: 2-4

Ingredients:

Rice, washed	2 cups / 400 gm
Clarified butter (*ghee*)	2 tsp / 10 gm
Cloves (*laung*)	4
Black cardamom (*bari elaichi*)	1
Water	4½ cups / 900 ml
Saffron (*kesar*) or yellow colour	a pinch
Sugar	1 cup / 200 gm

Method:

1. Heat the clarified butter in a wok (*kadhai*); add the cloves and black cardamom. Fry for 1-2 minutes.
2. Add the rice and mix. Pour in the water and edible colour or saffron. Cook until the rice is half done.
3. Mix the sugar and cook on a low heat until all the water evaporates and the rice is tender. Serve hot.

Just Rice

To protect rice from worms,
place a few garlic flakes in the container.

Malpua
Shallow fried pancakes soaked in sugar syrup

Preparation time: 45 min.
Cooking time: 20 min.
Serves: 4

Ingredients:

Toned milk	10 cups / 2 lt
Wholemilk fudge (*khoya*), grated (see p. 6)	4 tbsp / 60 gm
Refined flour (*maida*)	4 tsp / 20 gm
Cornflour	5 tsp / 25 gm
Green cardamom (*choti elaichi*) powder	½ tsp / 3 gm

For the sugar syrup:

Water	1¼ cups / 250 ml
Sugar	2½ cups / 500 gm
Vetiver (*kewda*) essence	1 tsp / 5 ml
Yellow colour	½ tsp / 3 ml
Clarified butter (*ghee*) for frying	

For the garnishing:

Pistachios (*pista*), blanched, chopped	4 tsp / 20 gm
Saffron (*kesar*)	a few strands

Method:

1. Boil the toned milk in a wok (*kadhai*) till it is reduced to ¼th.
2. Add the wholemilk fudge, reduce the heat to low and stir constantly till the fudge dissolves completely.
3. Remove from the heat into a mixing bowl and let the mixture cool. Add the refined flour, cornflour

Hot Desserts

and green cardamom powder and mix well to make a smooth batter.

4. For the sugar syrup, boil the water with the sugar in a pan and cook till the syrup reaches a thread-like consistency. Mix in the vetiver essence and the yellow colour.

5. Heat the clarified butter in a frying pan. Add one ladleful of batter and fry both the sides till golden brown.

Remove with a slotted spoon, drain the excess oil and immerse the pancakes directly into the sugar syrup. Repeat the same process until all the batter is used up.

6. Let the pancakes soak in the sugar syrup for a while.

7. Remove from the syrup and fold them into half. Arrange on a platter and serve hot, garnished with pistachios and saffron, and accompanied with *rabari* (see p. 48).

⇒

Say Cheese
*Put a pinch of sugar in the cheese box
to keep the cheese fresh and free from fungus.*

⇒

Lapsi
Sweet Rajasthani porridge

Preparation time: 15 min.
Cooking time: 30 min.
Serves: 4-6

Ingredients:

Broken wheat (*dalia*)	1 cup / 200 gm
Clarified butter (*ghee*)	½ cup / 100 gm
Aniseed (*saunf*)	1 tsp / 5 gm
Almonds (*badam*), blanched, halved	8-10
Dry coconut (*copra*), slivers	1 tbsp / 15 gm
Water	3 cups / 600 ml
Sugar	½ cup / 100 gm
Green cardamoms (*choti elaichi*), crushed	4

Method:

1. Heat the clarified butter in a wok (*kadhai*). Add the aniseed and let it crackle.
2. Add the broken wheat and stir-fry till it is well browned.
3. Add the almonds (keep a few aside for garnishing), dry coconut and water; bring to a boil.
4. Lower the flame and cook till the broken wheat becomes tender.
5. Add the sugar and stir till it dissolves completely.
6. Remove from the flame, garnish with green cardamom and the remaining almonds.

Parippu Payasam

South Indian green gram with coconut milk

Preparation time: 45 min.
Cooking time: 40-50 min.
Serves: 6-8

Ingredients:

Split green gram (*moong dal*) 2¼ cups / 250 gm
Coconut (*nariyal*) milk,
   second extract (see p. 7)   2 cups / 400 ml
Jaggery (*gur*), broken   3 cups / 600 gm
Coconut (*nariyal*) milk,
   first extract (see p. 7)   1¼ cups / 250 ml
Green cardamom
   (*choti elaichi*) powder   ½ tsp / 3 gm
Raisins (*kishmish*), fried   ¼ cup / 50 gm
Cashew nuts (*kaju*), fried   ¼ cup / 50 gm
Clarified butter (*ghee*)   5 tbsp / 75 gm

Method:

1. In a wok (*kadhai*), roast the split green gram to a light brown colour.
2. Pour in the second extract of the coconut milk and cook till the split green gram turns very soft.
3. Add the jaggery and cook till a thick consistency is obtained.
4. Now pour the first extract of the coconut milk and cook on a slow fire. Add the green cardamom powder and mix well. Remove from the fire.
5. Serve hot, garnished with raisins, cashew nuts and clarified butter.

Rawa Kesari

South Indian semolina flavoured with saffron

Preparation time: 40 min.
Cooking time: 25-30 min.
Serves: 6-8

Ingredients:

Semolina (*suji*), sieved	1¼ cups / 250 gm
Clarified butter (*ghee*)	1¼ cups / 250 gm
Saffron (*kesar*), soaked in lukewarm water	a few strands
Water	3¼ cups / 650 ml
Sugar	2½ cups / 500 gm
Green cardamom (*choti elaichi*) powder	1 tsp / 5 gm
Raisins (*kishmish*), fried	¼ cup / 50 gm
Cashew nuts (*kaju*), fried	¼ cup / 50 gm

Method:

1. Heat 50 gm of clarified butter in a pan. Add the semolina and fry for 10-15 minutes or till golden brown.
2. Add the saffron with the water and sugar. Cook till the water evaporates.
3. Add the remaining clarified butter and fry till the semolina mixture leaves the sides. Mix the green cardamom powder.
4. Serve hot, garnished with raisins and cashew nuts.

Imarti
Lentil roundels dipped in sugar syrup

Preparation time: 1 hr.
Cooking time: 30-40 min.
Serves: 4

Ingredients:

Lentil (*masoor dal*), washed,
soaked for 1 hour   1¼ cups / 250 gm
Yellow colour   1 tsp / 5 ml
Refined flour (*maida*)   5 tsp / 25 gm
Cornflour   5 tsp / 25 gm
For the sugar syrup:
Sugar   6¼ cups / 1250 gm
Water   7½ cups / 1½ lt
Saffron (*kesar*)   a few strands
Vetiver (*kewda*) essence   1 tsp / 5 ml

Clarified butter (*ghee*)   3¾ cups / 750 gm

Method:

1. Drain the lentil and blend to a coarse paste. Add the yellow colour, flour and cornflour. Keep aside.
2. For the sugar syrup, boil the water and sugar for about 20 minutes till the syrup reaches a thread-like consistency. Stir in the saffron and vetiver essence. Reduce the heat to low.
3. Heat the clarified butter in a shallow pan. Stuff the prepared paste into a cloth piping bag and pipe out the paste in circles, overlapping each other. Fry for 2-3 minutes on each side until golden yellow.
4. Remove and immerse the roundels directly into the hot sugar syrup. Let them soak for 2 minutes.
5. Remove, drain the excess syrup and serve hot.

Modur Pulao
Sweetened Kashmiri rice

Preparation time: 1 hr.
Cooking time: 40 min.
Serves: 4-6

Ingredients:

Basmati rice, washed, soaked for 1 hr	300 gm
Milk	5 cups / 1 lt
Sugar	2 cups / 400 gm
Clarified butter (*ghee*)	5 tbsp / 75 gm
Almonds (*badam*)	½ cup / 100 gm
Cashew nuts (*kaju*)	¼ cup / 50 gm
Raisins (*kishmish*)	¼ cup / 50 gm
Coconut (*nariyal*), diced	¼ cup / 50 gm
Cinnamon (*dalchini*), 1" sticks	3
Green cardamoms (*choti elaichi*)	6
Black peppercorns (*sabut kali mirch*)	6
Bay leaves (*tej patta*)	2
Saffron (*kesar*), soaked in ¼ cup water	2 gm
Cloves (*laung*)	6

Method:

1. Heat the milk in a heavy-bottomed pot. Add the drained rice and cook on a low flame till the milk begins to get absorbed. Remove from the flame, keeping the rice a little under done.
2. Transfer the rice to a large flat dish. Add the sugar and mix well gently.
3. Heat the clarified butter in a heavy-bottomed pot. Lightly fry the dry fruits, coconut, cinnamon, green cardamoms, peppercorns and bay leaves.
4. Add the rice and the saffron water. Stir well, gently.
5. Put a flat pan or griddle under the pot and cook covered, over a low flame till the rice is cooked. Garnish with cloves and serve hot.

Kashmiri Shufta
Dry fruits in sugar syrup

Preparation time: 30 min.
Cooking time: 15 min.
Serves: 10-15

Ingredients:

Cottage cheese (*paneer*), ½" cubes — 250 gm
Clarified butter (*ghee*) for frying
Clarified butter (*ghee*) — 2 tbsp / 30 gm
Almonds (*badam*), blanched — ½ cup / 100 gm
Raisins (*kishmish*) — ½ cup / 100 gm
Coconut (*nariyal*), slivered — ¼ cup / 50 gm
Dried dates (*khajoor*),
 deseeded, slivered — ¼ cup / 50 gm
Black peppercorns (*sabut kali mirch*) 1 tsp / 5 gm
Water — 1 cup / 200 ml
Sugar — 1½ cups / 300 gm
Green cardamoms (*choti elaichi*), crushed — 6
Saffron (*kesar*) — ½ tsp / 3 gm
Candied sugar (*misri*) — ¼ cup / 50 gm
Lemon (*nimbu*) juice — 1 tbsp / 15 ml

Method:

1. Heat the clarified butter (for frying) and fry the cottage cheese lightly. Remove and put aside.
2. Heat 2 tbsp of clarified butter in a pot. Lightly sauté the almonds, raisins, coconut, dried dates and black peppercorns for 1 minute.
3. Add water, sugar and green cardamoms. Stir till the water comes to a boil. Lower the flame and cook for 5 minutes.
4. Soak the saffron in 2 tsp of hot water, crush with the back of a spoon. Mix into the pot and stir well.
5. Add the candied sugar and lemon juice; stir again. When the syrup becomes thick (not dry), remove from the flame. Serve warm.

Gulab Jamun
Fried cottage cheese dumplings in sugar syrup

Preparation time: 20 min.
Cooking time: 2½ hrs.
Serves: 8-10

Ingredients:

Soft cottage cheese (*chenna*) (see p. 6)	4½ tbsp / 60 gm
Wholemilk fudge (*khoya*), grated (see p. 6)	2½ cups / 500 gm
Refined flour (*maida*)	4 tbsp / 60 gm
Baking soda	½ tsp / 3 gm
Water	2½ cups / 500 ml
Sugar	5 cups / 1 kg
Pistachios (*pista*), blanched, chopped	5 tsp / 25 gm
Saffron (*kesar*), soaked in 1 tbsp milk	¼ tsp / 1½ gm
Green cardamom (*choti elaichi*) powder	½ tsp / 3 gm
Oil	2½ cups / 500 ml

Method:

1. Rub the wholemilk fudge and cottage cheese together to a fine, creamy texture. Sieve in the flour and baking soda and knead to a soft dough. Divide into 20 balls and cover with a moist cloth.
2. Boil the water and sugar in a pan, removing the scum from time to time. Cook on a low heat till a thread-like consistency is obtained.
3. Make a thick paste of pistachios, saffron and green cardamom powder and divide into 20 portions.
4. Fill a portion into each of the cottage cheese balls.
5. Heat the oil in a pan; fry the dumplings over a low heat till golden. Remove with a slotted spoon and transfer into the sugar syrup. Leave in the syrup for at least 1-2 hours. Serve hot with the syrup.

Zauq-e-Shahi (Kala Jamun)

Fried dumplings served with thickened milk

Preparation time: 45 min.
Cooking time: 15 min.
Serves: 4

Ingredients:

Wholemilk fudge (*khoya*),
grated (see p. 6)   ½ cup / 100 gm
Soft cottage cheese (*chenna*),
(see p. 6)   4 tsp / 20 gm
Refined flour (*maida*), sieved   5 tsp / 25 gm
For the sugar syrup:
Water   ¾ cup / 150 ml
Sugar   1 cup / 200 gm

Clarified butter (*ghee*) for frying
Saffron (*kesar*)   a few strands
Pistachios (*pista*), chopped   4 tsp / 20 gm

*(See photograph on page 47, **extreme right**)*

Method:

1. Knead the wholemilk fudge, soft cottage cheese and flour into a smooth dough with a little water. Divide the dough into 20 equal-sized balls.
2. Make a thin sugar syrup by boiling the water and sugar together. Keep aside.
3. Heat the clarified butter in a wok (*kadhai*) on a low heat. Slide the balls and gently fry evenly on all sides. When the balls rise to the surface, increase the heat to moderate and cook till dark brown.
4. Remove, drain the excess oil and immerse in the sugar syrup. Let them soak till cool.
5. Spread a layer of *rabari* (see p. 48) on a serving dish and arrange the dumplings on top. Serve hot, garnished with saffron and pistachios.

Rabari

Vetiver and saffron flavoured thickened milk

Preparation time: 30 min.
Cooking time: 35 min.
Serves: 4

Ingredients:

Milk	5½ cups / 1½ lt
Wholemilk fudge (*khoya*), grated (see p. 6)	½ cup / 100 gm
Sugar	½ cup / 100 gm
Green cardamom (*choti elaichi*) powder	a pinch
Saffron (*kesar*)	a few strands
Pistachios (*pista*), blanched, chopped	4 tsp / 20 gm
Vetiver (*kewda*) essence	3-4 drops

Method:

1. Heat the milk in a wok (*kadhai*) on a moderate heat. Stir continuously till the milk is reduced to 1/5th.
2. Add the wholemilk fudge and cook on a very low heat for 2-3 minutes, stirring continuously, till the fudge dissolves completely.
3. Add the sugar and green cardamom powder and stir till the sugar is completely dissolved.
4. Remove from the heat and transfer into a serving dish. Keep aside to cool and refrigerate.
5. Serve garnished with saffron, pistachios and vetiver essence.

*(See photograph on page 47, **centre**)*

Makhane Ki Kheer
Sweet thickened milk with lotus seeds

Preparation time: 15 min.
Cooking time: 1½ hrs.
Serves: 4-6

Ingredients:

Lotus seeds (*makhane*)	1 cup / 200 gm
Water	1¼ cups / 250 ml
Milk	10 cups / 2 lt
Sugar	1 cup / 200 gm

Method:

1. Boil the lotus seeds in the water. Let them simmer for half an hour. Drain and keep aside.
2. Boil the milk in a wok (*kadhai*). Simmer for half an hour or till it becomes thick.
3. Add the lotus seeds and cook for about 5 minutes.
4. Add the sugar and stir till it dissolves completely. Remove from the fire and pour into a serving dish.
5. Serve chilled.

Note: Can also be served hot.

*(See photograph on page 47, **top left**)*

Chenna Payas

Soft cottage cheese dumplings in thickened milk

Preparation time: 45 min.
Cooking time: I hr.
Serves: 4-5

Ingredients:

For the soft cottage cheese (*chenna*):

Milk	12½ cups / 2½ lt
White vinegar (*safed sirka*) or lemon (*nimbu*) juice	2 tbsp / 30 ml

For the sugar syrup:

Sugar	2 cups / 400 gm
Water	1½ cups / 300 ml
Refined flour (*maida*)	5 tsp / 25 gm

For the thickenend milk:

Sugar	4 tbsp / 60 gm
Milk	5 cups / 1 lt
Green cardamom (*choti elaichi*) powder	½ tsp / 3 gm
Saffron (*kesar*)	2 gm
Almonds (*badam*), slivered	2 tsp / 10 gm
Pistachios (*pista*), slivered	2 tsp / 10 gm
Saffron (*kesar*)	a few strands

Method:

1. Boil the milk in a pan; add the white vinegar or lemon juice to curdle. Reduce the heat. Drain the whey and mash the curd cheese well. Keep aside.
2. For the sugar syrup, boil the water in a pot, add the sugar and stir continuously till the sugar dissolves completely.
3. Bring the syrup to a boil, lower the heat, add the refined flour and simmer. Allow to froth while the syrup is simmering.

4. Meanwhile, make 40 pellets from ¾ th of the curd cheese. Gently slide these into the syrup. Continue to simmer until they swell to double their size. Remove the dumplings from the sugar syrup with a slotted spoon and keep aside.

5. Cook the remaining curd cheese in a wok (*kadhai*) on a very low heat. Add the sugar and stir continuously. Cook till the mixture begins to leave the sides. Remove from the heat and keep aside to cool.

6. For the thickened milk, put the milk in a wok, bring to a boil and then simmer till it is reduced to ⅓ rd. Add the green cardamom powder and saffron; remove from the heat and stir in the above mixture.

7. Return to the flame and cook for about 10-12 minutes. Remove from the heat and keep aside to cool.

8. When cool, gently lower the dumplings into the mixture. Serve chilled, garnished with almonds, pistachios and saffron.

Easy Cut
Dry fruits can be easily cut by using scissors dipped in hot water.

Rasgulla

Soft cottage cheese dumplings in sugar syrup

Preparation time: 1 hr.
Cooking time: 4½ hrs.
Serves: 6-8

Ingredients:

Full-cream milk	10 cups / 2 lt
Lemon (*nimbu*) juice	4 tbsp / 60 ml
Water	10 cups / 2 lt
Sugar	7½ cups / 1½ kg
Cornstarch, dissolved in ¼ cup water	1 tbsp / 15 gm
Vetiver (*kewda*) essence	½ tsp / 3 ml

Method:

1. Boil the full-cream milk in a heavy-bottomed pan; reduce the heat and add the lemon juice to curdle. Remove from the heat and keep aside.

2. Pour the cheese-whey mixture into a moist cheesecloth. Pick up the cheesecloth by the corners, twist it loosely just to seal the cheese inside and rinse under the tap for a few minutes. Hang the cloth for 20-30 minutes to allow the excess water to drain.

3. Remove the cheese on a clear work surface and crumble it repeatedly till it becomes fluffy and smooth. Knead into a smooth dough and coat with a thin layer of oil on all sides. Divide the dough

into 16 portions and shape each portion into smooth balls. Keep aside.

4. Boil the sugar and water in a pan until the sugar dissolves completely. Cook on a high heat for 3-4 minutes. Then slide in the prepared balls. Increase the heat and boil continuously for about 20 minutes, adding the dissolved cornstarch after 4 minutes of boiling.

5. Add ¼ cup water to maintain the consistency of the syrup. Take care to add the water directly into the syrup and not on the balls. Remove from the heat.

6. Let the syrup cool for 10 minutes then sprinkle the vetiver essence. Leave the *rasgulla* to soak in the sugar syrup at room temperature for at least 4 hours. Serve chilled or at room temperature with the syrup.

Better Burfee

While preparing burfee *or* ladoo, *roast the gram flour in an oven. You will need less clarified butter and the taste will be far better.*

Pista Rasmalai

Soft cottage cheese patties in thickened milk

Preparation time: 1 hr.
Cooking time: 1½ hrs.
Serves: 4-5

Ingredients:

For the soft cottage cheese *(chenna):*

Milk	10 cups / 2 lt
Lemon *(nimbu)* juice	4 tbsp / 60 ml

For the cottage cheese balls:

Refined flour *(maida)*	4 tsp / 20 gm
Baking powder	¾ tsp / 3-4 gm
Water	4 cups / 800 ml
Sugar	4½ cups / 900 gm

For the thickened milk *(rabari):*

Full-cream milk	2½ cups / 500 ml
Sugar	½ cup / 100 gm

For the garnish:

Pistachios *(pista),* chopped	5 tsp / 25 gm
Saffron *(kesar),* dissolved in	
1 tbsp milk	¼ tsp / 1½ gm

Method:

1. For the soft cottage cheese, heat the milk in a pan and bring to a slow boil. Remove from the heat and let the milk cool for 5 minutes.
2. Add the lemon juice and stir till the milk curdles.
3. Carefully strain the curdled milk through a fine cheesecloth. Tie it up and let it hang for 30 minutes or until the liquid has completely drained off. The residue in the cheesecloth is cottage cheese.
4. Place the cottage cheese in a bowl, crumble with your fingers and rub till a creamy.
5. Sieve the flour and baking powder together; add the cottage cheese and knead to a fine, soft dough.
6. Divide the dough into 20 equal portions and flatten each slightly between your palms.

7. In a heavy pan, bring the water to a slow boil. Add the sugar, mix well over a low heat till completely dissolved to get a fine, clear syrup. Remove the scum from the surface.

8. Add the cottage cheese patties to the sugar syrup and boil on a low heat for 10 minutes or till they double in size and rise to the surface.

9. Remove the patties with a slotted spoon and keep aside for 3-4 minutes. Squeeze them gently to remove any syrup and place on a serving dish.

10. For the thickened milk, heat the milk on a low heat until reduced to half, stirring occasionally. Add the sugar, cool and refrigerate.

11. To serve, pour the chilled, thickened milk over the cottage cheese patties and cool in the refrigerator for at least 30 minutes. Garnish with pistachios and saffron.

Juicy Lemons
Soak dried lemons in boiling water
to make them soft and juicy.

Rajbhog
Cardamom-stuffed cottage cheese dumplings

Preparation time: 30 min.
Cooking time: 3 hrs.
Serves: 6-8

Ingredients:

For the filling:

Full-cream milk	1¾ cups / 350 ml
Sugar	2 tbsp / 30 gm
Pistachios (*pista*), grated	3 tbsp / 45 gm
Green cardamoms (*choti elaichi*), crushed	5

For the dumplings:

Full-cream milk	10 cups / 2 lt
Lemon (*nimbu*) juice	4 tbsp / 60 ml

For the syrup:

Water	10 cups / 2 lt
Sugar	7½ cups / 1½ kg
Cornstarch, dissolved in	
¼ cup water	1 tbsp / 15 gm
Rose water (*gulab jal*)	½ tsp / 3 ml

Method:

1. For the filling, boil the full-cream milk and sugar in a pan till the milk is reduced to half. Add the pistachios and green cardamoms; cook until the mixture leaves the sides of the pan. Keep aside.
2. For the dumplings, heat the milk over a high heat and bring to a boil. Reduce the heat and add lemon juice to curdle the milk. Remove from the fire.
3. Pour this cheese-whey mixture into a moist cheesecloth. Pick up the cheesecloth by its corners, twist it loosely just to seal the cheese inside and rinse under the tap for a few minutes. Hang the cloth for 20-30 minutes to allow the excess water to drain.

4. Remove the soft cottage cheese on a clean work surface and crumble it. Divide into 8 portions and flatten each slightly. Also divide the filling equally into 8 portions and place one in the centre of each patty. Roll into balls.

5. For the syrup, boil the sugar and water in a pan, till the sugar dissolves. Gently slide in the prepared balls. Boil for 20 minutes, adding the dissolved cornstarch to thicken the consistency of the syrup.

6. Remove from the flame and let the dumplings cool. Sprinkle rose water and serve chilled or at room temperature.

Pop and Thicken

If you wish to thicken the milk and are in a hurry, add some poppy seeds and watch the results!

Shahi Tukda Nawabi

Bread soaked in flavoured milk

Preparation time: 30 min.
Cooking time: 1 hr.
Serves: 4

Ingredients:

Milk	5 cups / 1 lt
Green cardamom	
(*choti elaichi*) powder	½ tsp / 3 gm
Saffron (*kesar*)	a few strands
Sugar	1½ cups / 300 gm
Clarified butter (*ghee*)	1 cup / 200 gm
Milk bread, slices	8

For the thickened milk (*rabari*):

Milk	10 cups / 2 lt
Sugar	½ cup / 100 gm
Green cardamom	
(*choti elaichi*) powder	½ tsp / 3 gm
Saffron (*kesar*)	a few strands
Almonds (*badam*), slivered	2 tsp / 10 gm
Pistachios (*pista*), slivered	2 tsp / 10 gm

Method:

1. Bring the milk to a boil in a heavy-bottomed pan. Add the green cardamom powder and saffron. Remove from the heat, add the sugar. Keep aside.
2. Heat the clarified butter in a pan; fry the slices of bread lightly. Remove, drain the excess oil. Soak the fried bread in the milk mixture for 10 minutes.
3. For the *rabari*, heat the milk and cook till it is reduced to ⅓rd. Stir in the sugar, green cardamom powder and saffron. Remove from the heat and keep aside to cool.
4. Carefully lift the slices of bread from the milk and place on a serving platter. Pour the *rabari* on top and garnish with almonds and pistachios.
5. Serve chilled or at room temperature.

Kheer
A rich creamy rice pudding

Preparation time: 1 hr.
Cooking time: 1 hr.
Serves: 4

Ingredients:

Milk	5 cups / 1 lt
Clarified butter (*ghee*)	2 tsp / 10 gm
Rice, long grain, washed, soaked for 1 hour	¼ cup / 50 gm
Sugar	½ cup / 100 gm
Green cardamom (*choti elaichi*) powder	1 tsp / 5 gm
Raisins (*kishmish*)	2 tsp / 10 gm
Almonds (*badam*), blanched, slivered	1 tbsp / 15 gm
Saffron (*kesar*), dissolved in 2 tbsp milk	a few strands

Method:

1. Boil the milk in a pot. In another pot heat the clarified butter; add the rice and stir-fry for 4-5 minutes till it begins to brown lightly.
2. Add the milk and bring the mixture to a boil, stirring constantly to prevent the rice from sticking. Simmer till the rice is cooked.
3. Stir in the sugar. Simmer till the milk thickens.
4. Add the green cardamom powder, raisins and almonds.
5. Sprinkle the saffron and serve hot in winter and cold in summer.

Sevain
Vermicelli milk pudding

Preparation time: 15 min.
Cooking time: 30 min.
Serves: 2-4

Ingredients:

Vermicelli (*sevain*)	1¼ cups / 250 gm
Clarified butter (*ghee*)	½ cup / 100 gm
Cloves (*laung*)	10
Green cardamoms (*choti elaichi*), seeds	11
Milk	6 cups / 1200 ml
Brown sugar	¾ cup / 150 gm
Almonds (*badam*), chopped	½ cup / 100 gm
Raisins (*kishmish*)	¼ cup / 50 gm
Rose water (*gulab jal*)	3 tsp / 15 ml

Method:

1. Heat the clarified butter in a wok (*kadhai*); add the cloves and green cardamoms. Sauté well for 2-3 minutes to release the aromatic oils into the clarified butter.
2. Add the vermicelli and fry for 2-3 minutes without breaking it. Add the milk and bring to a boil. While the milk is simmering, add the brown sugar stirring gently so that it dissolves. Cook for 15-20 minutes till the vermicelli becomes soft.
3. Mix the almonds and raisins and stir for another 5 minutes. Add the rose water. Stir till the mixture is thick, remove from the heat. Keep aside to cool.
4. Chill before serving.

Yel Adai
Coconut and rice pancakes

Preparation time: 20 min.
Cooking time: 20 min.
Serves: 2-4

Ingredients:

Rice, washed, soaked for 10-15 minutes	2½ cups / 500 gm
Water	2½ cups / 500 ml
Jaggery (*gur*)	1¼ cups / 250 gm
Coconut (*nariyal*), grated	1¼ cups / 250 gm
Clarified butter (*ghee*)	¾ cup / 150 gm
Salt to taste	
Green cardamom (*choti elaichi*), seeds	1 tsp / 5 gm
Banana leaves, cut into 4″ squares	4

Method:

1. To prepare the jaggery syrup, boil the water, add the jaggery and stir well. Remove the scum from time to time. Cook till the syrup is reduced to ¼th.
2. Add the coconut and cook for 5-8 minutes more. Stir in the clarified butter reserving about 25 gm.
3. Grind the rice with enough water to make a batter of dropping consistency. Add the salt and green cardamom seeds.
4. Smear the remaining clarified butter over the banana leaves. Place them over hot plates so that the leaves become soft. Pour the rice batter over the banana leaves, spread the jaggery mixture and fold in the shape of an envelope. Steam them for 18-20 minutes. Serve hot or cold.

Sikarni

Nepalese sweetened yoghurt

Preparation time: 1 hr.
Cooking time: 15 min.
Serves: 2-4

Ingredients:

Yoghurt (*dahi*), hung	2½ cups / 500 gm
Sugar	2 tbsp / 30 gm
Cinnamon (*dalchini*) powder	¼ tsp / 1½ gm
Green cardamom	
(*choti elaichi*) powder	½ tsp / 3 gm
Almonds (*badam*)-Pistachios (*pista*),	
peeled, finely sliced	1 tbsp / 15 gm
Raisins (*kishmish*)	1 tbsp / 15 gm
Saffron (*kesar*)	a few strands

Method:

1. Transfer the yoghurt to a bowl and add the sugar. Mix well until the sugar is dissolved.
2. Mix in the cinnamon and green cardamom powders. Chill thoroughly and serve in separate bowls, garnished with dry fruits and saffron.

Note: This is a kind of Shrikhand but different in taste. If desired, you can add a few chopped fruits (orange, banana, mango, etc.).

Kashmiri Phirun

Rice pudding

Preparation time: 4 hrs.
Cooking time: 1 hr.
Serves: 6-8

Ingredients:

Rice, cleaned	¾ cup / 150 gm
Milk	5 cups / 1 lt
Green cardamoms (*choti elaichi*), crushed	4
Almonds (*badam*), blanched, slivered	3¼ tbsp / 50 gm
Saffron (*kesar*)	a few strands
Sugar	1¼ cups / 250 gm
Clay bowls (*kasore*), soaked in water	8
Silver leaf (*varq*), for garnishing	

Method:

1. Soak the rice in water for 4 hours. Drain the water and let the rice dry. Then either crumble it or grind coarsely for 10 seconds.

2. Heat the milk in a heavy-bottomed pot. Bring to a boil; add the rice, green cardamoms and almonds. Stir frequently with a ladle.

3. Lower the flame and cook till the rice softens and the milk thickens. Stir continuously to ensure that the mixture doesn't stick to the bottom.

4. Crush the saffron and soak in a few spoons of hot milk. Add to the milk mixture followed by the sugar. Stir for a few minutes and remove from the flame.

5. Remove the clay bowls from the water, and let them dry. When the *phirun* is ready, serve in separate bowls. Decorate with silver leaf (optional) and serve chilled.

Mango Kulfi

Mango ice cream

Preparation time: 20 min.
Cooking time: 8½ hrs.
Serves: 6-8

Ingredients:

Mango (*aam*) pulp	2¼ cups / 450 gm
Milk	5 cups / 1 lt
Sugar	3 tbsp / 45 gm
Saffron (*kesar*)	a few strands
Cream (*malai*), thick	¾ cup / 150 ml

Method:

1. Boil the milk in a heavy-bottomed pan; lower the heat and let it simmer. Add the sugar and cook till the milk is reduced to ⅓rd and is thick and creamy.
2. Add the mango pulp and saffron; cook further for 2 minutes. Cool to room temperature and mix in the cream.
3. Spoon the mixture into 6-8 *kulfi* moulds. Seal tightly with silver foil and freeze for at least 8 hours. Shake the mould thrice during the first hour of freezing.
4. Just prior to serving, remove the moulds from the freezer. Dip the bottom of the moulds in hot water just for a few seconds to loosen the sides and invert on to serving dishes. Serve immediately.

Kujja Kulfi
Ice cream in earthenware moulds

Preparation time: 30 min.
Cooking time: 2 hrs.
Serves: 4

Ingredients:

Milk	5 cups / 1 lt
Sugar	4 tbsp / 60 gm
Saffron (*kesar*), soaked in 1 tbsp water	a few strands
Yellow colour	2-3 drops
Green cardamom (*choti elaichi*) powder	a pinch
Cashew nuts (*kaju*), chopped	4 tsp / 20 gm
Pistachios (*pista*), blanched, chopped	1 tbsp / 15 gm

Method:

1. Heat the milk in a wok (*kadhai*); cook on a medium heat, stirring constantly till it is reduced to ¼th.
2. Remove the milk from the heat and stir in the sugar till it is completely dissolved.
3. Mix in the saffron, yellow colour, green cardamom powder, cashew nuts and pistachios.
4. Fill the mixture into earthenware moulds (*kujja*), cover with a lid and seal with any dough.
5. Place the moulds in a freezer for 1½ hours to allow the mixture to set.
6. Remove from the freezer, take off the lid and serve immediately.

Pista Kulfi

Pistachio ice cream

Preparation time: 20 min.
Cooking time: 3 hrs.
Serves: 4-5

Ingredients:

Full-cream milk	20 cups / 4 lt
Sugar	2 cups / 400 gm
Pistachios *(pista)*, chopped	½ cup / 100 gm
Green cardamom	
(choti elaichi) powder	½ tsp / 3 gm
Cherries *(gilas)*, chopped	10

Method:

1. Boil the milk over a medium heat till it is reduced to half (30-45 minutes). The consistency should be slightly thick and the colour, a pale yellow.
2. Gradually, add the sugar. Stir for another 3-4 minutes until the sugar is completely dissolved.
3. Cool and add the pistachios, green cardamom powder and cherries.
4. Fill the mixture into *kulfi* moulds. Seal tightly with silver foil and freeze for 1½-2 hours.
5. Remove from the freezer, dip the bottom of the moulds in hot water just for a few seconds to loosen the sides, and invert on to the serving dishes. Serve with *falooda* (see p. 76).

Falooda

Fresh cornflour vermicelli served with kulfi

Preparation time: 10 min.
Cooking time: 30 min.
Serves: 4

Ingredients:

Water	2 cups / 400 ml
Cornflour	½ cup / 100 gm
Yellow colour (optional)	a few drops

Method:

1. Mix the water and cornflour in a wok (*kadhai*) and stir thoroughly. Add the yellow colour.
2. Cook on a low heat, stirring continuously, till the mixture thickens and becomes gelatinous. Remove from the heat.
3. Pour into a *falooda* press and place over a container filled with cold water.
4. Press the mixture out into a platter in one continuous stream without stopping.
5. Store the *falooda* in the refrigerator and serve chilled, as an accompaniment with *kulfi* (see p. 74). If desired, you can flavour the *falooda* with Roohafza or rose water.

(See photograph on page 75)

Shrikhand
Creamy yoghurt

Preparation time: 2-3 hrs.
Cooking time: I hrs.
Serves: 6-8

Ingredients:

Yoghurt (*dahi*), hung in a muslin
   cloth for 2-3 hours   7 cups / 1400 gm
Castor sugar   3 cups / 600 gm
Saffron (*kesar*), ground with
   1 tbsp vetiver (*kewda*) essence   a pinch
Green cardamom
   (*choti elaichi*) powder   12
Almonds (*badam*), blanched,
   peeled, sliced   20

Method:

1. In a serving bowl, mix the yoghurt with the castor sugar. Add the saffron mixture and the green cardamom powder. Beat well till a thick creamy consistency is obtained. Add half the almonds (keep the rest for garnishing).
2. Cover the bowl and chill in the refrigerator for at least 1 hour.
3. Serve garnished with the remaining almonds.

Chocolate Burfee

Chocolate fudge

Preparation time: 10 min.
Cooking time: 15 min.
Serves: 2-4
Calories per serving: approx 53

Ingredients:

Semolina (*suji*)	1 tbsp / 15 gm
Cottage cheese (*paneer*), from skimmed milk less than	1 cup / 100 gm
Cocoa powder	3 tsp / 15 gm
Artificial sweetener to taste or	8 tsp / 40 gm
Silver leaf (*varq*), optional	

Method:

1. Roast the semolina till golden. Grind if finer texture is required.
2. Knead the cottage cheese, cocoa powder, artificial sweetener and semolina paste together, add a little water if necessary.
3. Spread the mixture on a greased plate.
4. Cut and serve decorated with silver leaf (optional).

Saving Semolina

*Semolina (**suji**) will be free of worms*
if roasted for five minutes before it is stored.

Sandesh

Soft cottage cheese fudge

Preparation time: 20 min.
Cooking time: 15 min.
Serves: 2-4
Calories per serving: approx. 70

Ingredients:

Soft cottage cheese (*chenna*), from skimmed
milk, crumbled, (see p. 6) 1 cup / 100 gm
Sugar 2 tbsp / 30 gm
Rose water (*gulab jal*) ½ tsp / 3 ml
Artificial sweetener to taste
Cold water to knead
Raisins (*kishmish*), for garnishing
(optional) a few

Method:

1. Heat the sugar with 1 tbsp water till rich and
   caramel coloured. Add 1-2 tbsp water and remove
   from the flame.
2. Blend the caramel and soft cottage cheese in the
   blender. Add the rose water and artificial
   sweetener. Knead the mixture with cold water till
   soft and smooth.
3. Roll into small balls and flatten slightly. Place a
   raisin in the centre of each piece of fudge.
4. Serve at room temperature. When refrigerated, the
   fudge will stay for 3-4 days.

Apple Kheer
Apple pudding

Preparation time: 10 min.
Cooking time: 30 min.
Serves: 4-6
Calories per serving: approx. 109

Ingredients:

Apples (*seb*), puréed	500 gm
Cornflour	1 tbsp / 15 gm
Skimmed milk	3 cups / 600 ml
Raisins (*kishmish*)	4 tsp / 20 gm
Green cardamom (*choti elaichi*) powder	1 tsp / 5 gm
Nutmeg (*jaiphal*) powder	a pinch

Method:

1. Dissolve the cornflour in skimmed milk. Bring to a boil, stirring continuously. Cook for a few minutes till the milk thickens slightly.
2. Add the apple purée, raisins, green cardamom powder and nutmeg powder. Stir gently for a few minutes till the apple purée is cooked.
3. Serve chilled.

Apples Unpaired
Apples keep longer if they
do not touch one another.

Fruit Shrikhand

Creamy yoghurt with fruits

Preparation time: 1 hr.
Serves: 2-4
Calories per serving: approx. 85

Ingredients:

Yoghurt (*dahi*), hung for 1 hour	1 cup / 100 gm
Artificial sweetener to taste or	4 tsp / 20 gm
Green cardamom (*choti elaichi*) powder	¼ tsp / 1½ gm
Nutmeg (*jaiphal*) powder	a pinch
Mixed fruit (of your choice), puréed	150 gm
Lemon (*nimbu*) juice	2 tbsp / 30 ml
Artificial sweetener	2 tsp / 10 gm

Method:

1. Blend the yoghurt with the artificial sweetener and spices till creamy. Add a little water if necessary. Keep aside.
2. Mix the fruit purée with lemon juice and artificial sweetener. Keep aside.
3. Top the yoghurt mixture with the mixed fruit purée. Serve chilled.

Phirni

Rice pudding

Preparation time: 15 min.
Cooking time: 10 min.
Serves: 2-4
Calories per serving: approx. 80

Ingredients:

Skimmed milk	2 cups / 400 ml
Rice flour	1 tbsp / 15 gm
Almond (*badam*) essence	a few drops
Artificial sweetener to taste	
Green cardamom (*choti elaichi*) powder	½ tsp / 3 gm
Mixed cashew nuts-raisins (*kaju-kishmish*), chopped	2 tbsp / 30 gm

Method:

1. Dissolve the rice flour in the skimmed milk and cook till the milk thickens.
2. Blend the almond essence, artificial sweetener and green cardamom powder into the milk mixture.
3. Pour this mixture in a serving dish or individual clay bowls and chill. The *phirni* sets best in clay bowls.
4. Serve chilled, garnished with cashew nuts and raisins.

Moong Dal Kheer

Green gram pudding

Preparation time: 10 min.
Cooking time: 10 min.
Serves: 2-4
Calories per serving: approx. 130

Ingredients:

Split green gram (*moong dal*)	1 tbsp / 15 gm
Skimmed milk	1 cup / 200 ml
Green cardamom (*choti elaichi*) powder	¼ tsp / 1½ gm
Jaggery (*gur*), grated	1 tbsp / 15 gm
Coconut (*nariyal*), fresh, grated	1 tbsp / 15 gm
Artificial sweetener to taste or	4 tsp / 20 gm
Raisins (*kishmish*), chopped for garnishing	2 tsp / 10 gm

Method:

1. Roast the split green gram till golden brown; cool and powder coarsely.
2. Cook the powdered green gram with skimmed milk, green cardamom powder and jaggery till the green gram is soft and the mixture thickens a little.
3. Add the coconut and cook further for 1 minute.
4. Remove from the heat and add artificial sweetener.
5. Serve warm or chilled, garnished with raisins.

Makhane Ki Kheer
Lotus seed pudding

Preparation time: 10 min.
Cooking time: 5 min.
Serves: 2
Calories per serving: approx. 130

Ingredients:

Lotus seeds (*makhane*)	50 gm
Cornflour	1 tsp / 5 gm
Skimmed milk	1 cup / 200 ml
Green cardamom (*choti elaichi*) powder	¼ tsp / 1½ gm
Nutmeg (*jaiphal*) powder	a pinch
Artificial sweetener	4 tsp / 20 gm

Method:

1. Dissolve the cornflour in skimmed milk; bring to a boil. Cook for 1-2 minutes.
2. Dry roast the lotus seeds for a few minutes then add it to the milk mixture.
3. Stir in the green cardamom powder, nutmeg powder and artificial sweetener.
4. Serve chilled.

Peel Perfect
Add a little sugar before peeling cardamoms.
The peeling will be easier, after which, the seeds can be powdered.

Chenna Payas

Cottage cheese dumplings in thickened milk

Preparation time: 10 min.
Cooking time: 7 min.
Serves: 1-2
Calories per serving: approx. 115

Ingredients:

Soft cottage cheese (*chenna*), from skimmed milk (see p. 6)	1 cup / 100 gm
Cornflour	1 tsp / 5 gm
Skimmed milk	1 cup / 200 ml
Green cardamom (*choti elaichi*) powder	¼ tsp / 1½ gm
Artificial sweetener	4 tsp / 20 gm
Saffron (*kesar*), dissolved in warm milk	a few strands

Method:

1. Knead the soft cottage cheese well to make a smooth dough. Divide the dough into small balls. Keep aside.
2. Dissolve the cornflour in the skimmed milk, and bring to a boil.
3. Slide in the cottage cheese balls and cook for a minute or two.
4. Stir in the green cardamom powder, artificial sweetener and saffron.
5. Serve chilled.

Thandai
Frozen flavoured milk

Preparation time: 10 min.
Cooking time: 35 min.
Serves: 2-4
Calories per serving: approx. 70

Ingredients:

Skimmed milk	1 cup / 200 ml
Cornflour	1 tsp / 5 gm
Black pepper (*kali mirch*) powder	¼ tsp / 1½ gm
Poppy seeds (*khuskhus*), roasted, powdered	1 tsp / 5 gm
Aniseed (*saunf*), roasted, powdered	1 tsp / 5 gm
Rum	1 tbsp / 15 ml
Gelatine, dissolved in a little hot water	3 tsp / 15 gm
Artificial sweetener to taste or	4 tsp / 20 gm
Rose water (*gulab jal*)	¼ tsp / 1½ ml
Vetiver (*kewda*) essence	¼ tsp / 1½ ml
Almond (*badam*) essence	a few drops

Method:

1. Dissolve the cornflour in skimmed milk; add black pepper, poppy seed and aniseed powders and cook for 2-3 minutes till the milk thickens a little.
2. Remove from the flame, stir in the rum, gelatine mixture, artificial sweetener, rose water, vetiver and almond essences till well mixed.
3. Chill till set and serve.

Mango Kulfi

Mango ice cream

Preparation time: 15 min.
Cooking time: 10 min.
Serves: 4-6
Calories per serving: approx. 55

Ingredients:

Water, hot	1 cup / 200 ml
Gelatine, dissolved in	
2 tbsp hot water	2 tsp / 10 gm
Cornflour	2 tsp / 10 gm
Skimmed milk	1 cup / 200 ml
Papaya (*papita*), puréed	150 gm
Pistachios (*pista*), chopped	2 tbsp / 30 gm
Mango (*aam*) essence	¼ tsp / 1½ ml
Lemon (*nimbu*) juice	1 tbsp / 15 ml
Almond (*badam*) essence	a few drops
Vetiver (*kewda*) essence	a few drops
Saffron (*kesar*), soaked	
in 2 tbsp milk	a few strands
Orange food colour (optional)	a few drops
Artificial sweetener to taste or	8 tsp / 40 gm
Ice cubes	8-10

Method:

1. Heat the water in a pan; add the gelatine mixture. Stir till the gelatine is completely dissolved. Keep aside.
2. Dissolve the cornflour in skimmed milk, bring to a boil. Stir till the milk thickens slightly. Mix in the gelatine mixture; remove from the flame. Cool.
3. Add the remaining ingredients and blend till thick and creamy.
4. Freeze the mixture till it sets. Blend once again and refreeze in *kulfi* moulds before serving.

Sheera
Wholewheat flour porridge

Preparation time: 5 min.
Cooking time: 15 min.
Serves: 4-6
Calories per serving: approx. 63

Ingredients:

Wholewheat flour (*atta*)	3 tsp / 15 gm
Clarified butter (*ghee*)	1 tsp / 5 gm
Skimmed milk	3 cups / 600 ml
Green cardamom (*choti elaichi*) powder	¼ tsp / 1½ gm
Artificial sweetener to taste or	4 tsp / 20 gm

Method:

1. Roast the wholewheat flour with clarified butter till it is golden brown and the raw smell disappears.
2. Add the skimmed milk, stirring continuously to avoid the formation of lumps. Cook for a few minutes.
3. Stir in the green cardamom powder and add artificial sweetener to taste.
4. Serve hot or cold in silver or clay bowls.

Gur Dosa
Jaggery pancakes

Preparation time: 10 min.
Cooking time: 20 min.
Serves: 6-8
Calories per serving: approx. 140

Ingredients:

Jaggery (*gur*), grated	1 tbsp / 15 gm
Water	1 cup / 200 ml
Refined flour (*maida*)	75 gm
Rice flour, finely ground	25 gm
Lemon (*nimbu*)	½
Oil	4 tsp / 20 ml
Coconut (*nariyal*) powder	4 tsp / 20 gm
Artificial sweetener to taste (optional)	
Green cardamom (*choti elaichi*) powder	½ tsp / 3 gm
Clarified butter (*ghee*) or white butter	4 tsp / 20 gm

Method:

1. Put the jaggery in the water and let it dissolve. Add both the flours, a little at a time, and blend into a smooth batter.
2. Heat a small non-stick pan and rub the surface lightly with half a lemon dipped in very little oil. Pour a ladleful of batter, tilting the pan to help the mixture spread evenly. Sprinkle some oil and cook on both the sides till golden brown.
3. Mix the coconut powder with artificial sweetener and green cardamom powder. Sprinkle a little of this over the pancakes and roll into cylinders.
4. Brush each roll with ½ tsp melted clarified butter or top with ½ tsp lightly whipped white butter.
5. Serve warm.

Shahi Tukda
Slices of toasted bread with thickened milk

Preparation time: 5 min.
Cooking time: 10 min.
Serves: 2-4
Calories per serving: approx. 70

Ingredients:

Bread, slices	2
Clarified butter (*ghee*)	1 tsp / 5 gm
Water	2 tbsp / 30 ml
Rose water (*gulab jal*)	¼ tsp / 1½ ml
Artificial sweetener	6 tsp / 30 gm
Skimmed milk powder	2 tbsp / 30 gm
Almond (*badam*) / Pistachio (*pista*) essence	1-2 drops
Rose petals, for garnishing (optional)	

Method:

1. Toast the slices of bread in a pan with the clarified butter till golden in colour.
2. Add the rose water and 2 tsp artificial sweetener in the water; sprinkle the mixture over the slices of toasted bread. Cut each slice into quarters.
3. Mix the skimmed milk powder with almond or pistachio essence, the remaining artificial sweetener and a little water; blend till creamy. Spoon this milk mixture over the slices of bread.
4. Garnish with rose petals and serve chilled.

Poli
Stuffed Bengal gram pancake

Preparation time: 10 min.
Cooking time: 30 min.
Serves: 2-4
Calories per serving: approx. 180

I n g r e d i e n t s :

Refined flour (*maida*)	1 cup / 100 gm
Salt	a pinch
Bengal gram (*chana dal*)	75 gm
Artificial sweetener to taste	
Green cardamom	
(*choti elaichi*) powder	¼ tsp / 1½ gm
Clarified butter (*ghee*), melted	2½ tsp / 15 ml

M e t h o d :

1. Knead the flour and salt mixture into a soft dough with a little water. Divide the dough into 5 balls. Keep aside.

2. Roast the Bengal gram till golden and aromatic. Grind finely. Then pressure cook with ½ cup of water till soft.

3. In a non-stick pan, gently sauté the cooked Bengal gram till thick. Mix the artificial sweetener and green cardamom powder. Keep aside to cool. Divide the mixture into 5 equal portions.

4. Roll out each flour ball, dusting with flour, into a small round pancake. Place one portion of the Bengal gram mixture in the centre. Fold the pancake over the mixture shaping into a flattened ball again.

5. Roll out the filled dough into rounds as thinly as possible. Roast on a griddle (*tawa*) using ½ tsp clarified butter for each pancake.

6. Serve warm.

Gajar Ka Halwa
Carrot delight

Preparation time: 20 min.
Cooking time: 35 min.
Serves: 2-4
Calories per serving: approx. 112

Ingredients:

Carrots (*gajar*), grated	500 gm
Skimmed milk	3 cups / 600 ml
Raisins (*kishmish*), chopped	2 tsp / 10 gm
Artificial sweetener	8 tsp / 40 gm
Green cardamom (*choti elaichi*) powder	¼ tsp / 1½ gm
Clarified butter (*ghee*), melted	2 tsp / 10 gm

Method:

1. Cook the carrots with skimmed milk in a large heavy-bottomed pan till the milk evaporates.
2. Remove from the flame; add raisins, artificial sweetener and green cardamom powder. Mix well.
3. Serve warm or chilled, topped with ½ tsp clarified butter per serving.

Selecting Carrots
*The deeper the colour of carrots,
the better the source of vitamin A.*

Glossary of Cooking Terms

Batter	—	A mixture of flour, liquid and sometimes other ingredients, of a thin, creamy consistency.
Blend	—	To mix together thoroughly two or more ingredients.
Caramel	—	Sugar heated to a rich brown coloured syrup.
Curdle	—	To cause milk or a sauce to separate into curds and whey in the presence of acid or excessive heat.
Dropping consistency	—	If a spoonful of mixture is lifted from the bowl, it should drop off the spoon in 5 seconds.
Knead	—	To work a dough by hand or machine until smooth.
Purée	—	Fruit, meat or vegetables pounded, sieved or pulverised in an electric blender.
Sift	—	To shake a dry ingredient through a sieve to remove lumps.
Syrup	—	A concentrated solution of sugar in water.

Index

ISBN: 81-7436-156-1

© **Roli Books Pvt. Ltd. 2001**
Lustre Press Pvt. Ltd.
M-75, Greater Kailash-II Market,
New Delhi-110 048, INDIA
Phones: (011) 6442271, 6462782, 6460886
Fax: (011) 6467185, E-mail: roli@vsnl.com
Website: rolibooks.com

Photographs:
Dheeraj Paul, Neeraj Paul and Deepak Budhraja

Printed and bound in Singapore